LIGHT AND
SOUND

SCIENCE
FACT FILES

LIGHT AND
SOUND

Steve Parker

RAINTREE
STECK-VAUGHN
RSVP® PUBLISHERS

A Harcourt Company

Austin • New York
www.steck-vaughn.com

Produced by Roger Coote Publishing

Published by Raintree Steck-Vaughn, an imprint of Steck-Vaughn Company

Design and typesetting Tim Mayer and Victoria Webb
Project Editor Lisa Edwards
Editor Steve Setford
Picture Researcher Lynda Lines
Illustrators Alex Pang and Michael Rosen

Raintree Steck-Vaughn Staff:
Editor Pam Wells
Project Manager Max Brinkmann

Parker, Steve.
    Light and sound / Steve Parker.
        p. cm. -- (Science fact files)
    Includes bibliographical references and index.
    ISBN 0-7398-1011-1
    1. Light--Juvenile literature. 2. Sound--Juvenile literature.
    [1. Light. 2. Sound.] I. Title. II. Series.

QC360. P65 2000
535--dc21   00-031074

Pages 2–3: Light from brilliant fireworks brightens the sky.
Title page picture: The artificial beam from a lighthouse
is outshone by natural lighting.

We are grateful to the following for permission to reproduce photographs: Digital Stock 36 bottom (Marty Snyderman); Digital Vision *front cover background and bottom right*, 9, 15, 34; Science Photo Library *front cover top right*, 8 left (Alex Bartel), 8 bottom (Martin Bond), 11 bottom (Keith Kent), 12 bottom (G Antonio Milani), 14 (Cortier/BSIP), 16 (Jerome Wexler), 18 top (Alfred Pasieka), 20 (Claude Nuridsany & Marie Perennou), 21 (Omikron), 22 (David Scharf), 26 (Robert Holmgren/Peter Arnold Inc), 27 (Phillippe Plailly/Eurelios), 28 top and bottom left (Philippe Plailly), 28 bottom right (David Parker), 30 (Will & Deni McIntyre), 32 (Volker Steger), 33 (US Air Force), 36 top (Carlos Munoz-Yague/Eurelios), 37 (Dr Morley Read), 38 Prof P Motta/La Sapienza), 39 both (Prof C Ferlaud/CNRI), 42 (Dr Jeremy Burgess),43 bottom (CS Langlois/Publiphoto Diffusion); The Stock Market 11 top (John Martin), 12 top (Sanford/Agliolo), 18 bottom, 35 top (Milt & Patti Putnam), 43 top (Torlief Svensson); Tony Stone 25 (Robert E Daemmrich), 31 (Tom Raymond), 35 bottom (Demetrio Carrasco).

The statistics given in this book are the most up to date available at the time of going to press.

Printed in Hong Kong

0 1 2 3 4 5 6 7 8 9 WKT 05 04 03 02 01 00

CONTENTS

INTRODUCTION

Though we rarely think about light and sound, they are always present and vital to so many aspects of our daily lives. We need them to find our way around, stay safe, communicate, learn about the world, and enjoy ourselves.

Light and sound are crucial to science, technology, industry, and medicine. There are innumerable machines and gadgets based on light and sound, from the flashing, wailing sirens of an ambulance or police car to the medical ultrasound scanners that provide images of unborn babies, the industrial **laser** beams that cut through steel, and the giant telescopes that probe the mysteries of the universe.

HISTORY FILE

THE TRUE NATURE OF LIGHT

Long ago, people thought we could see because light shone out of our eyes and illuminated our surroundings. But one thousand years ago the Persian scientist Alhazen (c. AD 965 – c.1038) turned this around by suggesting that light originates from a source, such as the Sun or a candle, and bounces off the objects around us into our eyes. He was right. Alhazen also studied color, mirrors, and lenses. His book on the science of light, *The Treasury of Optics*, was the best on the subject for five hundred years.

Wave energy

In some ways, light and sound are similar. They are both forms of **energy**, which is the ability to make things happen, do work, produce activity or cause change. In both light and sound, the energy travels as waves, moving from place to place in the form of up-and-down or back-and-forth **vibrations**.

Light from dazzling fireworks brightens the night sky.

All waves are forms of energy. Wave generators turn ocean wave energy into electricity.

FACT FILE

PROPERTIES OF WAVES

• Waves spread out from their source in all directions, unless they are blocked, redirected or absorbed by something.

• The highest part of a wave is called the crest. The lowest part is known as the trough.

• A wave curves above and below an imaginary horizontal line through its middle. This line is the midline or equilibrium.

• All waves of the same kind travel at the same speed in the same substance. All sound waves, for example, travel at 340 meters (1,115 ft)/s in air.

• Waves usually change speed when they go from one substance to another, such as when light waves pass from air to water.

• The height of a wave is called the amplitude. It is the distance from the midline up to the crest, or from the midline down to the trough.

• The distance from a point on one wave to the same point on the next wave, such as from crest to crest or trough to trough, is called the **wavelength**.

• The number of waves that pass in one second is called the **frequency**. It is measured in units called **Hertz (Hz)**.

• Waves eventually fade as their **energy** disperses.

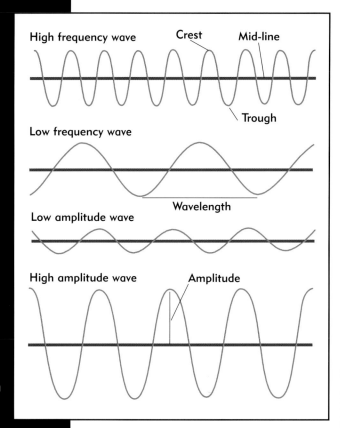

As the length of a wave decreases, its frequency increases.

A wave is a type of regular change, or disturbance, from the normal. A pond's surface, for example, is normally flat. If a stone is dropped into it, waves spread out in the form of ripples in the water. A rope normally lies flat. If one end is flicked hard, waves "chase" each other along the rope (see page 31).

Despite both traveling as waves, light and sound have many differences. For a start, they are different forms of energy. They also move at very different speeds. Sound needs matter—a gas such as air, a liquid such as water, or a solid such as wood—to be able to travel. Light, on the other hand, can travel in a **vacuum** (a complete absence of matter). The vast, open reaches of deep space are a near-vacuum, where there is nothing more substantial than a few specks of dust. So you would be able to see the blazing rockets of a nearby spaceship, but you would not be able to hear them.

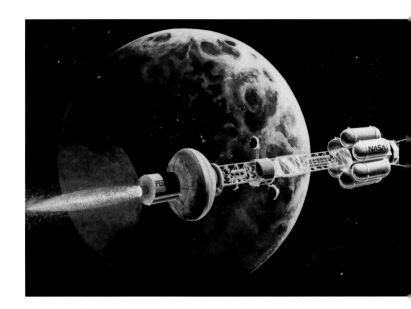

Light waves travel through space, but sound waves cannot.

9

WHAT IS LIGHT?

Light is easy to see but difficult to describe. It is a form of energy called **electromagnetic (EM) radiation**, which consists of ripples, or waves, of electricity and magnetism combined. As well as light, there are many other types of electromagnetic radiation, including radio waves, microwaves, infrared waves, ultraviolet rays, X rays and gamma rays. Together, they form the electromagnetic spectrum. All the waves in the spectrum travel in the same way and at the same speed. But they differ in their wavelengths and frequencies, from long, low-frequency radio waves to incredibly short, high-frequency gamma rays.

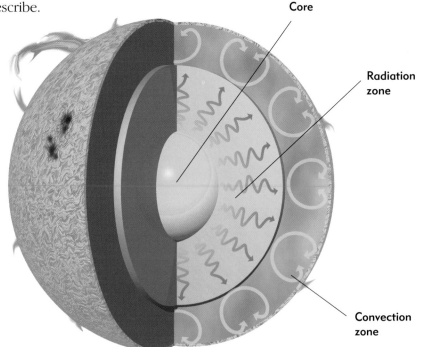

Core

Radiation zone

Convection zone

Light for our world

Our main light source is the Sun, a vast, glowing, 5-billion-year-old ball of burning hydrogen and helium gas 150 million kilometers (93 million miles) away. Sunlight is vital to life on Earth. Without it, there would be no plant life, because plants fuel their growth by capturing the energy of sunlight in a process called photosynthesis. And without plants, there would be no animal life, because all animals feed either on plants or on other animals that are plant-eaters.

Nuclear reactions at the center of the Sun produce vast amounts of gamma-ray energy. By the time this energy reaches the surface, it has mostly changed to heat and light, which travels out into space. Some of it reaches the Earth.

FACT FILE

POLARIZED LIGHT

In ordinary light, the waves vibrate in many different directions, but in **polarized light**, all the waves vibrate in the same direction. A polarizing filter makes unpolarized light into polarized light by allowing waves that vibrate in only one direction to pass through it. Polarizing filters are used in sunglasses to reduce glare.

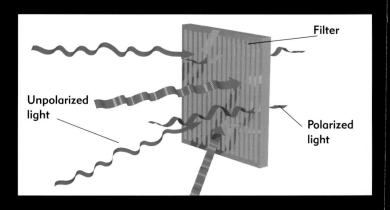

Filter

Unpolarized light

Polarized light

The polarizing filter stops all waves of light except those vibrating in a certain direction.

A lighthouse beam flashes on and off to warn ships and boats about rocks, cliffs, and dangerous waters.

Light production

The production of light by hot objects—such as the Sun's surface, a burning candle or a glowing wire—is called incandescence. Some substances absorb light or other energy briefly and then give it out again as light without getting hot. This is called fluorescence. Fluorescent chemicals are used in detergents to make clothes look brighter. Other substances, such as glow-in-the dark-paints, absorb light or other energy and gradually release it as light over a longer period. This is called phosphorescence.

Animal light

Some animals are bioluminescent, which means that they can produce their own light. These creatures include deep-sea fish, such as anglerfish, lantern fish, and flashlight fish, and certain sponges, shrimps, jellyfish, and coral animals. On land there are fireflies, cave insects, even shining slugs. The light is usually used to attract mates or to lure prey. There are also types of fungi that glow, such as foxfire.

HISTORY FILE

LIGHTING OUR WAY
• c.500,000 BC: people first tamed fire for light, warmth, and cooking.
• c.13,000 BC: oil lamps were first used.
• c.1000 BC: wax candles lit Greek and Roman dwellings.
• c. AD 1800: lamps fueled by natural gas were used to light city streets.
• 1808: arc lights, which use electric sparks to make an intense light, were invented.
• 1879: the electric filament bulb, which heats a wire so it glows, was developed by Thomas Edison (1847–1931) in the U.S. and Joseph Swan (1828–1914) in England.
• 1930s: the fluorescent tube, developed in the 1890s by French physicist Antoine Henri Becquerel (1852–1908), became widespread. It produces light by passing electricity through a gas.
• 1950s: bright colored neon lights for advertising became common. Like fluorescent tubes, they use electricity to make a gas glow with light.
• 1980s: compact fluorescent bulbs, which use less electricity than filament bulbs, became available as low-cost electric lights.

Fireflies, actually types of beetles, show as faint green streaks of light.

TRAVELING LIGHT

The speed of light in a vacuum, which is about 300,000 kilometers (186,000 mi)/second is the fastest possible speed. Nothing at all, anywhere in the universe, can exceed it. So in the near-vacuum of space, nothing is faster or straighter than light. However, here on Earth, things are very different, and many objects and substances get in the way of light rays. Light also travels slower when it passes through matter. For example, in water the speed of light falls to 225,000 kilometers (139 mi)/s and in glass it travels at about 185,000 kilometers (115,000 mi)/s.

Transparent substances

Exactly what happens when light rays strike an object or substance determines how the object or substance appears to our eyes. For example, substances such as air, window glass, lake water, and plastic wrap let light pass through them virtually unhindered. We see through these substances clearly. They are called transparent.

Translucent substances

Other substances let light rays pass through, but change the direction of the light in a random way, scattering the rays. These substances are translucent. They include frosted glass, cloudy water, fog and mist, and tracing paper. We can see the light's brightness through these substances, but the view is hazy.

Unhindered, light always travels in straight lines like these sunbeams.

Opaque substances

A substance that blocks the path of light rays completely, letting no light pass through at all, is said to be opaque. The light rays are either absorbed by the substance or bounce off it. Opaque substances range from rocks, soil and wood, to metals, some plastics and living things such as dogs, cats, and ourselves. We cannot see through an opaque object, instead we see the object itself.

This view of city lights from a hilltop shows how fog scatters the light rays.

HISTORY FILE

WAVES OR PARTICLES – OR BOTH?
The Dutch scientist Christiaan Huygens (1629–1693) first suggested that light consists of traveling waves of energy. Other scientists, especially Isaac Newton (1642–1727) in England, said that light was made up of tiny particles of energy. Today, scientists accept both ideas. Light sometimes acts as if it is electromagnetic waves, and sometimes as if it is a stream of tiny packets of energy called photons.

Shadows

Because light rays travel in straight lines, they cannot bend round an opaque object in their path. This leaves a dark area on the other side of the object, known as a shadow. Most shadows have two regions. The umbra is the dark central part, where the object has blocked out all the light. The penumbra is the lighter area around the umbra, where some rays have reached but not others.

Eclipses

The Moon sometimes comes between the Sun and the Earth, blocking the path of the Sun's light rays heading towards the Earth. This casts a shadow of the Moon on the Earth's surface. From the Earth, we see a solar eclipse, in which the Moon covers up the bright disk of the Sun. At other times, the Earth comes between the Moon and the Sun and gets in the way of sunlight heading for the Moon. The Earth casts its shadow onto the Moon, which appears to "go out," leaving only a dark disc in the sky. This is called a lunar eclipse.

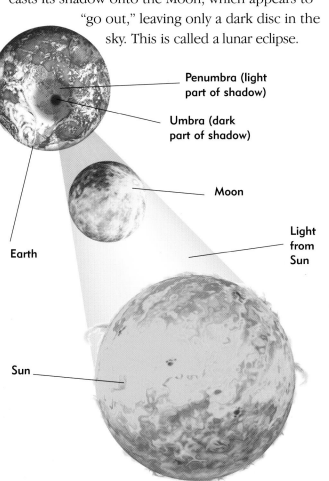

Penumbra (light part of shadow)

Umbra (dark part of shadow)

Moon

Earth

Light from Sun

Sun

TEST FILE

MAKE A SUNDIAL

Long ago, people used sundials to tell the time from the shadows cast by the Sun.

• Use a sheet of cardboard for the base of the sundial. From another sheet, cut a right-angled triangle. This is called the gnomon.

• Tape the gnomon to the base by one of its shorter sides, so that the gnomon stands upright in the middle of the base.

• Early on a clear day, put the sundial in a sunny place. Use a magnetic compass to align the card triangle north-south, with the upright (vertical) side facing north.

• Every hour, draw a line from the gnomon's base along the edge of the shadow cast by its upright side. Label the line with the time.

• On the next day, you will be able to tell the time using the sundial.

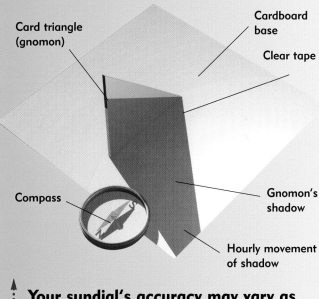

Card triangle (gnomon)

Cardboard base

Clear tape

Compass

Gnomon's shadow

Hourly movement of shadow

Your sundial's accuracy may vary as the Sun's path across the sky changes with the seasons.

In a solar eclipse, the Moon passes between the Sun and the Earth.

BOUNCING LIGHT

We see some objects, such as the Sun, a candle, a lightbulb or a TV screen, because they are light sources. They actually produce light themselves. All other objects, such as a tree, a pencil or this book, are visible because rays from a light source bounce off them and into our eyes. This bouncing is called **reflection**.

Mirror images

Most objects have rough surfaces. When light rays strike them, the rays are scattered, bouncing off the surface in all directions. But other surfaces, such as polished metal or calm water, are very flat, smooth, and shiny. They reflect light in an organized way, in the same pattern as it reaches the surface. We call these surfaces mirrors, and the images we can see on their surfaces are reflections, or mirror images.

When we look in a mirror, the brain assumes that the light rays have reached our eyes by traveling in a straight line. So the image we see appears to be behind the mirror.

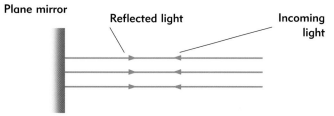

Plane mirror
Reflected light
Incoming light

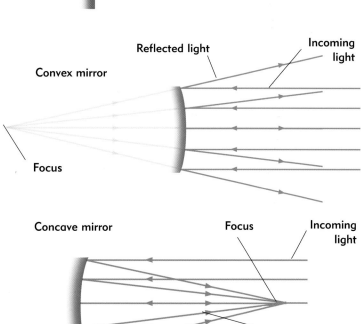

Convex mirror
Reflected light
Incoming light
Focus

Concave mirror
Focus
Incoming light
Reflected light

Flat and curved mirrors reflect light rays in different ways.

Types of mirrors

A plane or flat mirror produces an accurate, undistorted image of a scene or object. Plane mirrors are used in ordinary wall mirrors, and in devices such as kaleidoscopes and periscopes. Curved mirrors reflect light in such a way that they alter the view we see in them. The waves of light converge (come together) at a certain point, called the **focus**, to give a clear but changed image.

A convex mirror curves outwards, towards the viewer. It produces a smaller, wide-angle image of an object or scene, so that things appear farther away than they really are. Rear-view mirrors in cars are often convex, to give a broad view of traffic behind.

A concave mirror curves inwards, away from the viewer. It produces a magnified image, so that things appear closer than they are in reality. Makeup and shaving mirrors are concave, to give close-up or enlarged views of your face.

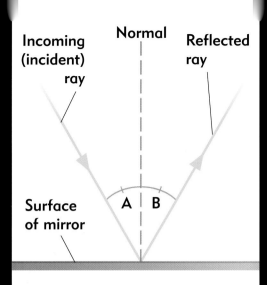

Incoming (incident) ray

Normal

Reflected ray

Surface of mirror

A | B

FACT FILE

LAW OF REFLECTION
When light rays reflect off surfaces, they follow the scientific rule known as the law of reflection. This involves an imaginary line called the normal, which is at 90° to the reflecting surface. The law states that the angle between the incoming light ray and the normal is the same as the angle between the reflected light ray and the normal. So in the diagram, angle A = angle B. The law of reflection was known to the Persian scientist Alhazen (see page 8) about one thousand years ago.

Internal reflection

If a light ray in a transparent substance such as glass hits the inside surface of the glass at a shallow enough angle, it may become trapped inside the glass. Instead of leaving, the light ray is repeatedly reflected back and forth between the inner surfaces of the glass. This is called total internal reflection.

Optical fibers

Total internal reflection is used in optical fibers. An optical fiber is a long, hair-thin rod of special glass or plastic. A beam of light is shone into the end of the rod. The beam hits the rod's inner surface at a shallow angle and then undergoes total internal reflection. It travels on, and does the same again. In this way, light zigzags along the inside of the fiber, even when the fiber bends around a corner.

FUTURE FILE

LIMITLESS INFORMATION?
Cables containing optical fibers are used to send telephone calls, computer data, or TV programs as flashes of laser light (see pages 26–27). A fiber-optic cable can carry 10,000 times more information than an electrical cable of the same thickness. As fiber-optic technology advances, these amounts will increase. The only limit on them may be the speed of light itself.

An optical fiber (fiber optic) carries light rays even around curves and corners.

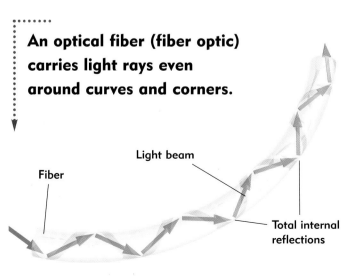

Fiber

Light beam

Total internal reflections

A fiber-optic cable contains thousands of individual optical fibers.

BENDING LIGHT

As light passes from one transparent substance to another, such as from air into water, or water into glass, it changes speed. The sudden change of speed bends the light waves. This bending is called **refraction**. It is why fish sometimes seem to be closer to the water's surface than they really are, and why a straw standing in a glass of water appears to break apart where it enters the water.

Lens images

A lens is a piece of transparent material, such as glass or plastic, with curved surfaces. Light refracts going into and out of the lens in such a way that it alters the view through the lens. As with curved mirrors, the rays of light converge at a point called the focus to give a clear but changed image. The distance from the focus to the center of the lens is known as the focal length. Thicker lenses are more powerful than thinner ones and have shorter focal lengths.

We know the straw is not broken. But refraction makes it look like it is.

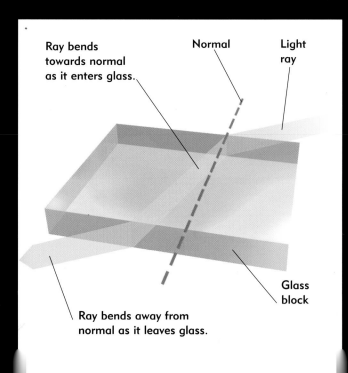

FACT FILE

LAW OF REFRACTION
When light rays refract, they follow the law of refraction. Like the law of reflection, it involves an imaginary line— the normal—at 90° to the refracting surfaces. The law states that a light ray bends towards the normal as it passes from air into a transparent substance at an angle. It bends away from the normal when it leaves the substance and passes back into air. The law of refraction was devised in 1621 by Dutch scientist Willebrord Snel (1580–1626).

Ray bends towards normal as it enters glass.

Normal

Light ray

Glass block

Ray bends away from normal as it leaves glass.

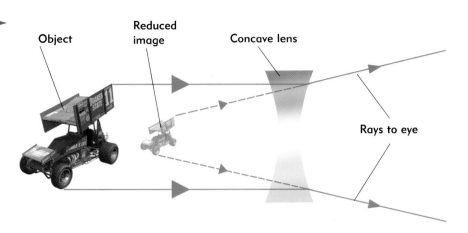

A concave lens bends light rays out as they shine into the eye, which makes the object appear smaller.

Object

Reduced image

Concave lens

Rays to eye

Concave lenses

A concave lens curves inward, so that it is thinner in the middle than at its edges. Light rays passing through the lens are made to diverge (bend away from each other), producing a reduced, wide-angle image of an object or scene. Concave lenses are used in cameras to squeeze a large, broad scene—such as a wide landscape view—into a small photograph.

Convex lenses

A convex lens bulges outward, so that it is thicker in the middle than at its edges. Rays of light passing through the lens are made to converge (bend towards each other) and form an image of an object or scene. This may be a magnified or reduced image, depending on the distance of the object from the lens. Convex lenses are used in microscopes, hand lenses, binoculars, telescopes, and other devices that make objects appear nearer or bigger.

The Fresnel lens is a special type of convex lens, developed by the French physicist Augustin Jean Fresnel (1788-1827). The surface of the lens is cut

into a series of stepped rings, one inside the other. It is used in lighthouses, searchlights, and car headlights to concentrate light into a strong beam.

Mirages

In hot places, you can sometimes see what appears to be a shimmering reflection of an object in a pool of water, when there is really no water there at all. This is a mirage, and it occurs when light rays are refracted by a layer of warm air close to the ground. Light rays bouncing off the object travel straight to your eyes, as they would normally. But rays traveling from the object to the ground are bent upward and into your eyes by the warm air. From far away it looks as if the object has a watery reflection beneath it.

A convex lens works as a magnifier to enlarge the image.

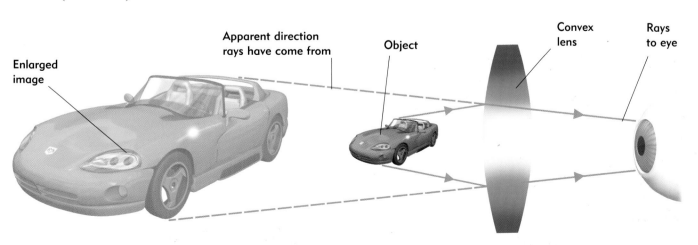

Enlarged image

Apparent direction rays have come from

Object

Convex lens

Rays to eye

COLOR AND BRIGHTNESS

The idea of light as waves of electromagnetic radiation (see page 10) helps to explain its various properties. For example, a bright light source gives out taller waves with bigger amplitudes than a dim light source. Colors can also be explained in terms of waves.

Hidden colors

Hold a red transparent piece of plastic wrapping paper up to your eyes. Look through it and everything appears red. Do the same with a blue piece. Now everything seems blue. Likewise, the scene is green when viewed through a green piece. This happens because ordinary daylight, or "white" light as it is known, contains many different colors. Each different color is electromagnetic radiation with a slightly different wavelength. The piece of plastic works as a color filter. It absorbs certain colors of light, but lets others pass through. For example, the red wrap cuts out all colors except red, which it lets through. The red light reaches your eyes, so the wrapper and view look red.

Splitting light

Ordinary white light can be split into all of its colors by a prism—a triangular block of glass or plastic. As a ray of white light enters the prism, it slows down.

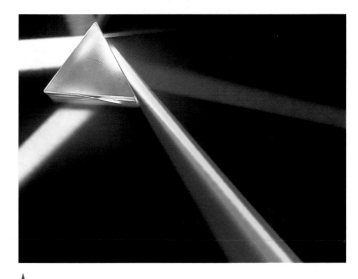

A prism of glass splits white light into all of its colors—the spectrum.

The sudden change of speed refracts, or bends, the light waves. But each color in the white light bends by a slightly different amount. Red light has the longest wavelength and bends the least. Green light has shorter waves and is bent more. Violet light has the shortest wavelength and is bent the most.

A beam of white light fans out as it passes through the prism and separates into a band of colors called a **spectrum**. The spectrum's seven

MIXING COLORS
Colored pigments
• There are three primary (main) colors of pigments. These are magenta, cyan, and yellow.
• All the other colors of pigments can be obtained by mixing these three primary pigment colors in varying proportions.
• For example, cyan and yellow together make green, and so on.
• All three primary pigment colors mixed together make black.

Colored lights
• There are three primary (main) colors of light. These are red, green, and blue.
• All the other colors of light can be obtained by mixing these three primary light colors in varying proportions.
• For example, red added to green makes yellow, and so on.
• All three primary light colors added together make white.

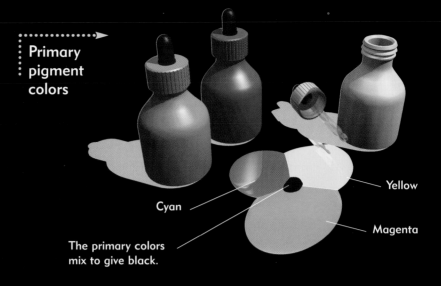

Primary pigment colors

Cyan

Yellow

Magenta

The primary colors mix to give black.

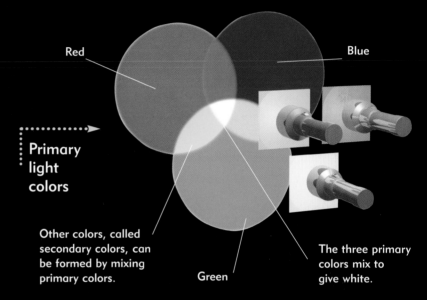

Red

Blue

Primary light colors

Other colors, called secondary colors, can be formed by mixing primary colors.

Green

The three primary colors mix to give white.

main colors always appear in the following order: red, orange, yellow, green, blue, indigo, and violet.

Rainbow colors
When it rains on a sunny day, stand with your back to the Sun. As the Sun's white light shines on raindrops in the air, each drop works like a tiny prism, splitting up the white light into the colors of the spectrum. Seen from afar, the spectra produced by millions of raindrops merge to form a large curved band of colors across the sky—a rainbow.

Raindrops work as natural prisms to make the spectrum we call a rainbow.

Why objects have color
Some objects, such as the yellow flames of a fire or the blue flames of a gas burner, appear colored because they give out light of a particular color. However, objects that do not produce light themselves get their color in a different way. When white light falls on them, they absorb some of the colors in the white light and reflect the others. Green plants, for example, look green because they absorb all the colors of white light except one, green, which they reflect.

Pigments are substances used to give color to paints, inks, and dyes and they work in the same way. A red ink, for example, reflects red light and absorbs all other colors. Likewise, a blue ink absorbs all colors except blue.

SEEING LIGHT

Compared to many other animals, humans have good eyesight. The human eye can detect movements and details quite well and has excellent color vision. It can even see reasonably well in dim light, such as at dusk.

Inside the eye

The human eyeball is a sphere about 2.5 cm (1 in) across that sits in a bony socket in the skull. It is protected by a tough white outer layer called the sclera. At the front of the eye, the sclera is domed and transparent, and is called the cornea. Light passing through the cornea is refracted so that it enters the eye through the pupil—a dark hole surrounded by a colored ring of muscle called the iris. The iris alters the size of the pupil, making it smaller in bright conditions to prevent too much light from entering the eye and damaging its delicate interior. In dim conditions, the iris makes the pupil wider to enable more light to enter the eye and help you see better.

The lens and focusing

After entering the eye, light rays pass through a clear convex lens that focuses them so that they form an image at the back of the eye. The shape of the lens is changed by the ciliary muscles that surround it. When you look at something close up, the light rays that enter your eye are diverging, so they need to be refracted a great deal in order to form an image. To

A fly's eye contains many single light-sensing units. Each picks up light from only a small part of the total view.

do this, the ciliary muscles contract and make the lens fatter and more rounded. When you look at a distant scene, the light rays are almost parallel as they enter your eyes, so they do not need to be refracted much. In this case, the muscles relax so that the lens flattens out.

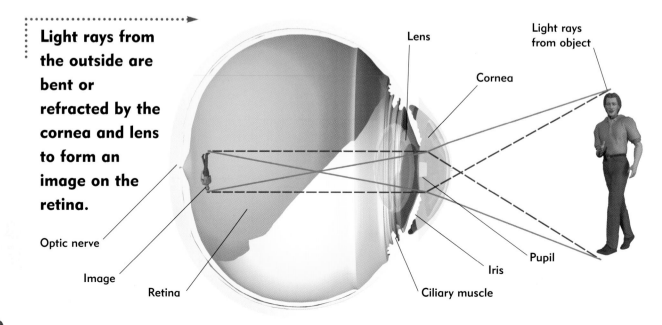

Light rays from the outside are bent or refracted by the cornea and lens to form an image on the retina.

Optic nerve

Image

Retina

Lens

Cornea

Light rays from object

Pupil

Iris

Ciliary muscle

FACT FILE

NEAR OR FAR?

We judge distances using a combination of methods:

- **Block:** Nearer objects are in front of and block out farther ones.
- **Relative size:** The farther away an object is, the smaller it appears. If a rabbit and a man look the same size, the rabbit is closer.
- **Accommodation:** The brain senses how much the lens's ciliary muscles pull to change its shape when focusing. The more pull, the thicker the lens and so the closer the object is.
- **Stereoscopic vision:** Each eye sees an object from a slightly different angle. The brain compares the two views. The nearer an object is, the more the two views differ.
- **Convergence:** The brain senses how the eyes swivel inward, or converge, when looking directly at an object. The more they converge, the nearer the object is.
- **Parallax:** Move your head from side to side and see how nearby objects seem to pass across distant ones.
- **Haze and fade:** Tiny bits of dust in the air make faraway things seem hazy and blurred, and colors faded and less bright.

The retina and light detection

The focused light rays form a postage-stamp-sized image on the lining at the back of the eye, known as the **retina**. Light-sensitive cells in the retina fire off nerve signals when they detect the light rays. The signals travel from the rear of the eye along the optic nerve to the sight centers at the back of the brain. The image that forms on the retina is actually upside down, because the light rays cross over inside the eye. The brain interprets the image so that we see things the right way up.

The retina has two kinds of light-sensitive cells, called rods and cones. The 125 million rods are sensitive to shades of black and white and can detect movement. The 7 million cones detect colors and enable you to see things in detail. Unlike rods, cone cells do not work in dull light.

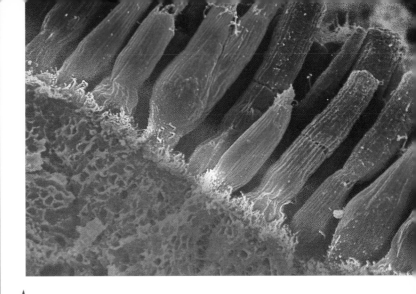

The retina has more than 130 million microscopic light-detecting cells.

When the eyes confuse the brain

We think of optical illusions as things that play tricks on our eyes. In fact, they trick the brain. The eye records what it sees and passes on the information to the brain, which tries to make sense of the images. Most optical illusions can exist only in two dimensions—that is, on paper and not as objects in real life. The brain tries to understand them as real, three-dimensional objects, and so gets tricked.

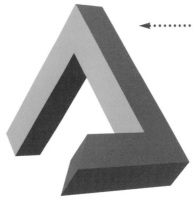

The tribar, an optical illusion, consists of three sections joined by right angles.

Seen from another angle, the tribar seems to form a triangle, even though this would be impossible in a 3-D shape.

USING LIGHT

Devices that work using light are called optical instruments. A simple hand lens has a convex lens that makes light rays from an object converge before they reach your eyes (see page 17). When you look through the lens, you see an image of the object that makes it seem much larger and closer than it really is. Hand lenses have many uses, including helping partially-sighted people to read small print in books, forensic scientists to study fingerprints, and biologists to identify insects.

Microscopes

Scientists use microscopes to produce magnified, detailed images of tiny objects or creatures. A microscope magnifies in two stages, using a pair of convex lenses inside a closed tube. There is a main magnifying lens called the objective and a viewing lens called the eyepiece. The object to be examined, the "specimen," is mounted on a glass slide and placed below the objective lens. A mirror reflects light up through the specimen and into the powerful objective lens. This forms an enlarged image of the specimen, which is further magnified by the eyepiece.

FACT FILE

TELESCOPES AND MICROSCOPES
- The world's biggest refractor telescope is at Yerkes Observatory, Wisconsin. Its objective lens is 116 cm (46 in) across.
- The world's biggest single-mirror reflecto telescope is at Mount Semirodriki, Zelenchukskaya, Russia. The mirror is abou 600 cm (236 in) in diameter.
- The most powerful light microscopes magnify objects up to about 2,000 times.
- More powerful microscopes do not use light waves, but beams of particles called electrons. Some electron microscopes can magnify more than one million times.

This blood-sucking mite is magnified to almost 200 times its real-life size.

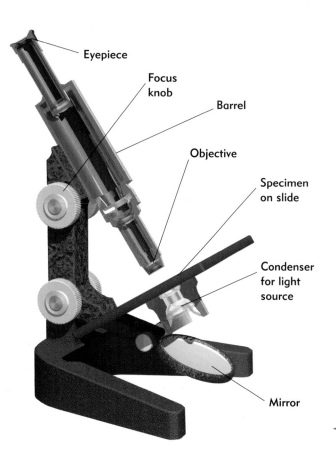

Eyepiece

Focus knob

Barrel

Objective

Specimen on slide

Condenser for light source

Mirror

A standard light microscope can magnify about 500-1,000 times.

Telescopes

Telescopes form magnified images of distant objects, enabling astronomers to see deep into space. There are two types of telescopes, called refracting and reflecting telescopes. As light rays enter a refracting telescope, a convex objective lens bends them to form an enlarged, upside-down image. A convex eyepiece lens bends the light rays again, magnifying the image for the observer. The main difference between a microscope and a refracting telescope is in the focusing power (focal length) of the objective lens. In a microscope the focal length is much shorter than in a telescope, because greater focusing power is needed to magnify close objects.

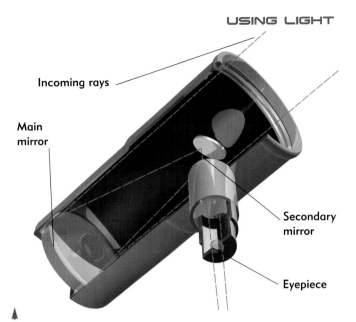

Incoming rays

Main mirror

Secondary mirror

Eyepiece

A reflecting telescope uses a curved mirror rather than a large lens.

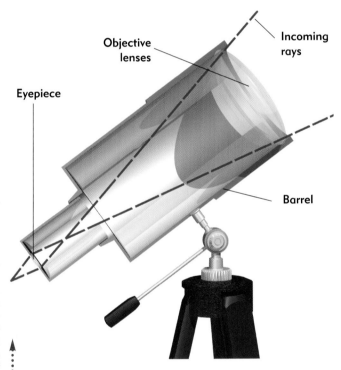

Objective lenses

Incoming rays

Eyepiece

Barrel

A refracting telescope has a large lens or multiple lens system at the front.

A reflecting telescope uses a concave mirror instead of an objective lens, focusing the light rays to form an image on a flat, angled mirror. This second mirror reflects the image into a convex eyepiece lens that magnifies it. The largest astronomical telescopes use mirrors rather than lenses, because they are easier to manufacture and install.

Binoculars

Binoculars consist of a pair of compact refracting telescopes joined together. A telescope has a long tube because a long distance is needed between the objective and eyepiece lenses to obtain a high magnification. In binoculars, this distance is reduced by inserting prisms between each objective and eyepiece lens. The prism reflects light rays back and forth, "folding up" the light rays and increasing the magnification possible in each short binocular tube.

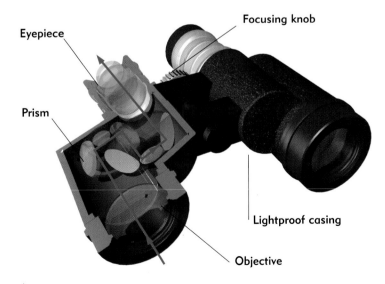

Focusing knob

Eyepiece

Prism

Lightproof casing

Objective

Binoculars "fold" the light rays so they can be shorter than a telescope.

CAMERAS AND PHOTOGRAPHS

A camera takes a picture by capturing the patterns of light from a scene on a light-sensitive surface such as photographic film. A lens focuses light rays entering the camera onto the film. Between the lens and the film are a variable-sized hole called an aperture and a fast-acting shutter, which control the amount of light entering the camera. When light shines onto the light-sensitive chemicals coating the surface of the film, they react together and change into different chemicals. Developing the film makes these changed chemicals visible. The result is a record of the pattern of light as it shone onto the original film—a photograph.

Still pictures

In many cameras, the shutter opens and closes very quickly, capturing a scene as it appears in a small instant in time—usually between one-hundredth and one five-hundredth of a second. Because the shutter is open for such a short time, most things in the photograph look still or stationary, except for very fast-moving objects such as cars, trains, and planes. These appear blurred, because they are traveling so quickly that their images move across the film while the shutter is open.

Shutter button · Batteries · Prism · Light rays into eye · Mirror · Film · Lenses

In this camera the mirror swings up to let light rays shine onto the film.

HISTORY FILE

STILL PHOTOGRAPHY
1816: Frenchman Joseph Niepce (1765–1833) recorded a rooftop scene on photographic film. It was a negative image, in which light areas appeared dark, and dark areas light.
1826: Niepce made the first positive photograph, in which light and dark appear correctly. No copies could be made.
1839: Englishman William H. Fox Talbot (1800–77) devised a process for making lots of positive copies from one negative.
1884: In the U.S., George Eastman

(1854–1932) put photographic chemicals onto flexible rolls of film, rather than the rigid plates that had been used previously.
1891: Frenchman Gabriel Lippman (1845–1921) made the first color photographs.
1947: American Edwin Land (1909–91) invented the first instant camera, which contained its own developing chemicals to produce photographs almost immediately.
1982: The Sony corporation of Japan produced the first electronic camera.

TV cameras in the studio show us moving pictures.

Moving pictures

A movie camera does not really record moving images, as its name implies. It takes a very rapid succession of still photographs, such as one every twenty-fifth of a second, on a roll of movie film. These individual photos are called frames. When the frames are shown in a movie projector at the same speed, they appear to our eyes to merge into continuous movement.

This happens because it takes each rod or cone cell in our eyes up to one-tenth of a second to receive light rays, produce a nerve signal, send this to the brain, and prepare for more light rays. A succession of still photographs shown faster than this seem to merge together as one moving scene.

Television works in the same way, showing 25 or 30 frames per second. If a movie film or TV set is slowed down to about ten frames per second, our eyes can keep up with the changes and we see them as a series of flickering still pictures.

Chemical-free cameras

In most video cameras and some still cameras, the light-sensitive surface is not photographic film, but a light-sensing microchip called a charge-coupled device, or CCD. This changes the pattern of light rays into patterns of tiny electrical signals, just as the human eye does when it looks at a scene and sends messages to the brain. The signals from the CCD are stored as tiny patches of magnetism on a magnetic tape (videotape) or disk. These images do not need to be chemically developed. Instead, the tapes can be put into a video player and played back immediately, while the disks can be put into a computer and the images shown on a monitor.

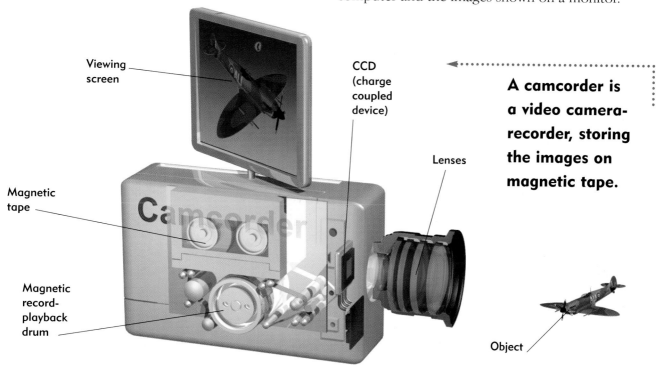

Viewing screen

CCD (charge coupled device)

Lenses

Magnetic tape

Magnetic record-playback drum

Object

A camcorder is a video camera-recorder, storing the images on magnetic tape.

LASER LIGHT

As we have seen, ordinary white light consists of waves of many different lengths, which we know as colors. These waves do not rise and fall in step with each other. They spread out in all directions from their source.

Laser light is different. All the waves in laser light are the same length, giving a single, pure color. They are also coherent, which means that they rise and fall together, exactly in step. And they are in line or parallel, and do not spread out from their source.

These features give beams of laser light special powers. They can be so strong and intense that when they shine on an object, their energy turns rapidly to heat and makes the object warm up, melt, or even burst into flames.

Making a laser beam

Laser means Light Amplification by Stimulated Emission of Radiation, which sums up how a laser works. Inside a laser is a substance called an active medium. This may be a solid, such as a rod of ruby crystal, a liquid, or even a gas. Energy in the form of flashes of light, heat, or pulses of electricity is fed into the active medium. This gives the atoms or molecules of the active medium extra energy, making them vibrate faster and faster. Eventually, they become so stimulated that they give off their excess energy as tiny particles of light, which are called photons.

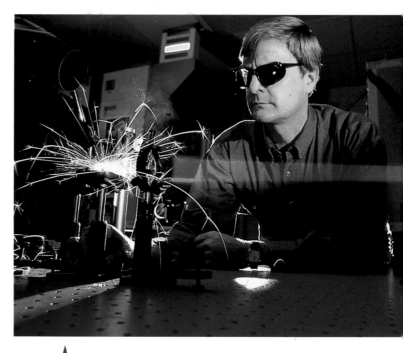

Industrial laser beams are so intense that they can cut through or weld together metals.

The photons released by the active medium form a beam of light, which reflects back and forth between mirrors at either end of the laser, becoming more and more intense. Eventually, the beam is so intense that it escapes through one of the mirrors, whose surface is only partly reflecting. It emerges as laser light.

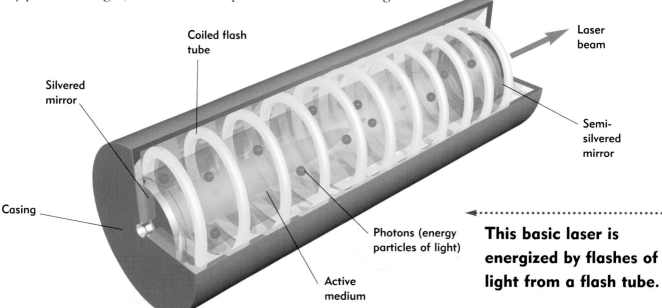

Coiled flash tube

Laser beam

Silvered mirror

Semi-silvered mirror

Casing

Photons (energy particles of light)

This basic laser is energized by flashes of light from a flash tube.

Active medium

The power of the laser

High-powered, computer-controlled industrial laser beams are used to cut complicated shapes from sheets of textiles, plastics, and even metals with great accuracy. Low-powered laser beams are used in hospitals to make tiny, delicate cuts in operations. The beam can also be focused to make a "hot-spot" a certain distance away. This does not affect the surface of the body where the beam touches it, but makes a cut inside the body, such as within the eye.

Tiny laser beams also cut or etch electronic components into silicon to make microchips, which are widely used in electronic devices. In a compact disk player, a tiny red laser beam reads coded information from a disk.

To the Moon and back

Because laser beams stay straight and narrow for enormous distances, astronomers use them to measure the distance to the Moon. A laser beam

Laser beams fired from Earth to the Moon reflect back from the Moon and measure the distance to within 2 cm (.78 in).

is shone at a mirror on the Moon (placed there by astronauts) and reflected back to Earth. The time for the beam to return is measured extremely precisely, to within millionths of a second. Knowing the speed of light, astronomers can then make accurate calculations of the distance to the Moon.

Useful laser-rulers

Laser beams are also used as very long, straight rulers in mapmaking, surveying, and construction. They measure distances across lakes and mountain ranges, detect land movements that may warn of earthquakes and volcanoes, and help to line up large structures such as tunnels, bridges, skyscrapers, and dams.

FACT FILE

LASERS AND THEIR USES

Lasers are described by the substance used for their active medium, which also determines how they are used.

Carbon dioxide gas: Cutting, melting, and welding in industry and medicine.

Argon ion gas: Cutting and heat-treating metals; making and viewing **holograms** (see pages 28–29).

Silicon diode semiconductor: Making and reading compact discs; used in fiber-optic communications.

Neodymium glass or crystal: Controlling nuclear reactions in power stations; cutting and welding; used in laser-guided weapons.

Helium-neon gas: Taking measurements for mapmaking, surveying, and construction; making and viewing holograms.

HOLOGRAMS

An ordinary picture on a flat surface, such as a painting or photograph, has two dimensions: height and width. You cannot look around or behind the objects in the picture. A hologram is also a picture on a flat surface, but it has three dimensions: height, width, and depth. Because it is a three-dimensional (3-D) image, you can see around objects in the picture and behind them. A hologram is a type of photograph made with laser light.

Interference

Holograms work by **interference,** that is, the way waves interact with each other when they meet. If you add one light wave to another wave of equal wavelength, the result depends on whether the waves are in step or not. If the two waves are exactly in step, with their crests and troughs lined up, then they add together to form a single wave with higher crests and lower troughs than the original two waves. If the two waves are exactly out of step, with the crests of one corresponding with the trough of the other, then the two waves cancel each other out. The result is hardly any wave at all. This interference occurs with all forms of waves, including sound waves.

Holograms are difficult to forge or fake, so they are used for pictures on credit cards and security passes.

Interference patterns

In light, interference happens when light waves are reflected or refracted from two surfaces that are very close together, or by tiny repeating lines, holes, or slots. Interference occurs as the waves meet, producing light and dark patterns. If the light is white light containing many different colors, some colors are canceled out, while others are made brighter. The result is a rainbow effect, or iridescent sheen that can be seen on soap bubbles, compact disks, thin films of oil, and butterfly wings.

Holograms look like real solid objects, but they are just patterns of light.

Interference makes soap bubble patterns.

How holograms are made

To create a hologram, a laser beam is shone into a device called a beam splitter that divides the beam in two. The two beams are then spread out by lenses. One, the reference beam, shines directly onto light-sensitive holographic film (similar to photographic film). The other, the object beam, shines onto the object being photographed, and is then reflected onto the holographic film.

The film does not record a normal image of the object. Instead, it records the interference patterns made when the reference and object beams come together. Close up, this looks like nothing more than a huge maze of tiny spots, stripes, and lines. But when the interference pattern is viewed correctly, it re-creates a realistic 3-D view of the original object. One way of viewing it is through a transparent cover with tiny ridges. Another way is in a beam of light similar to the original laser beam, or in polarized light.

A hologram is made when a split laser beam records interference patterns.

FUTURE FILE

USING HOLOGRAMS

Holograms already have a wide range of uses, but they will become much more widespread in the future:

• They can be used to record complex 3-D structures such as underground cave systems, valuable sculptures or jewels, rooms in a large building, or the pipes, wires, cables, and tunnels under a city.

• Optical computers will use laser light pulses instead of electrical signals, and work much faster. They will have crystal-based holographic memory chips that could increase the speed and storage capacity of computers by many thousands of times.

• One day, each person may have his or her own hologram ID (identity) card or cube, containing personal details such as medical records, photos, and full life history!

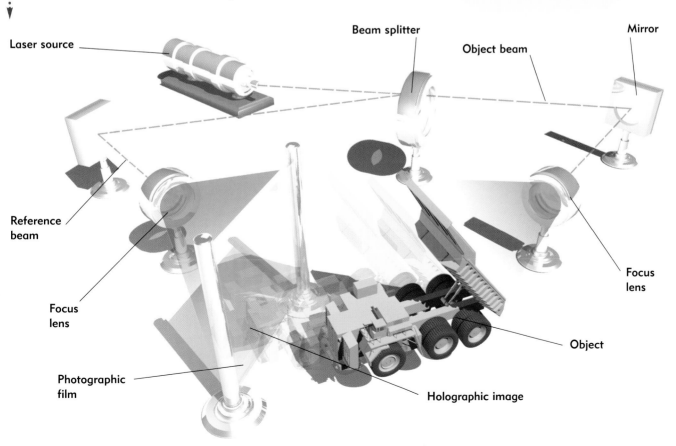

Laser source

Beam splitter

Object beam

Mirror

Reference beam

Focus lens

Focus lens

Object

Photographic film

Holographic image

WHAT IS SOUND?

ike light, sound is a form of wave energy. Whereas, light waves are a form of energy that we can see; sound waves are a form of energy we can hear. Sound travels as waves of vibration through the atoms and molecules that make up substances. As each atom or molecule vibrates, it bumps into those around it, transferring its energy and making them vibrate as well. This is why sound cannot travel in a vacuum, where there are no atoms or molecules to pass on the energy.

Pressure waves

Sound waves are produced when an object is made to vibrate, such as when you bang a drum. The vibrating skin of a drum, for example, sets off back-and-forth vibrations among the atoms and molecules of the surrounding air. The sound waves ripple outward from their source and through the air.

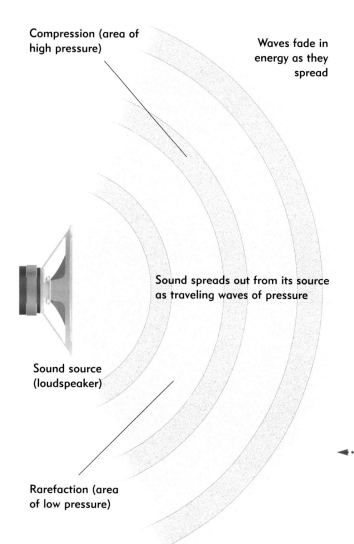

Compression (area of high pressure)

Waves fade in energy as they spread

Sound spreads out from its source as traveling waves of pressure

Sound source (loudspeaker)

Rarefaction (area of low pressure)

Sounds from inside the body can indicate illness or disease.

Like other types of waves, sound waves have crests and troughs. Each crest of a sound wave is an area of high pressure, called a compression, where the atoms and molecules are squeezed closer together than normal. Each trough of a wave is a low-pressure area, called a rarefaction, where the atoms and molecules are farther apart than normal. So sounds travel through the air as alternating regions of high and low air pressure.

Sound waves ripple out in all directions from their source.

Going nowhere

Imagine a cork floating on a pond's surface. As ripples or waves go past it, the cork bobs up and down. But the cork and the water around it do not travel along with the crests of the wave. This shows how the water waves transmit energy, while the water that the waves travel in moves very little.

A similar thing happens with sound waves. The areas of high and low air pressure move outward from the source, but the atoms and molecules that make up the air only move or vibrate by a very small amount. Even in the loudest sounds, these atoms and molecules vibrate by less than one-tenth of one millimeter (0.0003 in) from their normal positions.

A huge range of sound waves, loud and soft, with low and high notes, comes from an orchestra or band.

TEST FILE

MAKING WAVES

• Lay a length of rope on the ground. Flick one end hard. Watch how a wave travels along the rope as an up-and-down, or vertical, movement. This is a transverse type of wave, like light waves.

• Flick one end of a spring or coil sideways. Watch how a wave travels along the spring as back-and-forth or sideways, movements of its coils. This is a longitudinal type of wave, like sound waves.

• Stretch a sheet of plastic wrap tightly over a saucepan or baking pan. Sprinkle grains of flour, salt, or sugar on the plastic wrap. Hold a baking tray nearby and bang it hard with a wooden spoon. Sound waves from the tray pass through the air, hit the film, make it vibrate and shake the grains. Invisible sound has visible effects!

TRAVELING SOUND

The atoms and molecules of a gas, such as air, are relatively far apart compared with those in liquids and solids. In a sound wave, they have a comparatively long way to move before they bump into neighbors and make them vibrate. In fact, they are so far apart that some may never bump into other atoms and molecules. Not only that, the atoms and molecules are also continually swirling around in air currents. This is why sound waves soon fade in air, and why a strong wind can "blow sounds away."

Sounds in solids and liquids

A liquid is different. Its atoms and molecules are closer together. When they vibrate as part of a sound wave, they are more likely to—and sooner to—bump into neighbors. So sounds tend to travel farther and faster in liquids than they do in gases.

Firm, rigid solids, such as a steel bar, are even better at transmitting sounds, because their atoms and molecules are packed tightly together in orderly patterns. This is why the noise of an approaching train can be heard coming from the steel tracks long before it is heard through the air.

Architects test different materials for their sound-absorbing qualities.

Not all solids are so sound-friendly. In soft, spongy or floppy solids, including plastic foam, natural fibres like cotton and artificial fibers like nylon, the energy of sound waves is soaked up or absorbed very quickly. The sound waves bounce around in the gaps within the material, getting scattered and gradually weaker.

FACT FILE

SPEEDS OF SOUND

When people talk of the "speed of sound," they are usually referring to the speed at which sound travels in air. This is about 344 meters (1,129 ft)/sec at sea level. But because the air gets colder and less dense with height, sound's speed falls to about 295 m (968 ft)/sec at an altitude of 10,000 m (133,000 ft).

Below are the speeds of sound in other substances under normal conditions—in meters (feet) per second):
• Pure water: 1,498 m (4915 ft)/s
• Sea water: 1,531 m (5023 ft)/s

A supersonic aircraft breaks the sound barrier.

Air pressure waves build up at front

Sound waves spread out behind to give sonic boom

THE SOUND BARRIER

The first person to travel faster than sound was U.S. Air Force Captain Charles, "Chuck," Yeager (1923–). On October 14, 1947, he piloted a bright orange rocket plane, the Bell X-1, and "broke the sound barrier" high over California. Today many military planes fly faster than sound—some more than three times faster. The only commercial airliner to break the sound barrier regularly is the Anglo-French Concorde that can reach speeds of 2,130 km (11,324 mi)/h.

Reflected sounds

Like light waves, sound waves bounce, or reflect, off hard surfaces. The reflected sound waves are called an **echo**. The harder and smoother the surface, the clearer and louder the echo. Shout or clap in front of a large wall, and you will hear an echo of the noise a short while later. The farther you stand from the wall, the longer the echo takes to reach you. Most of the sounds that we hear are not "pure sounds," but a combination of the original sound and echoes bouncing off nearby objects like walls and floors.

Searching with sonar

Sounds travel fast and far in water. A sonar system sends out pulses of sound waves through water and detects any returning echoes. From the time it takes to send out the sound waves and receive the echoes, a computer works out the distance to the object that has reflected the sounds. From the direction, pattern and strength of the echoes, it can work out the position, size, and even shape of the object.

The word *sonar* stands for SOund Navigation And Ranging. It is also called echo sounding or echolocation. Various animals have developed their own natural sonar. In the oceans, some whales, dolphins, and seals are able to produce high-pitched clicks and squeaks and detect the returning echoes. They use their sonar to communicate, find food, and navigate. In air, bats and some cave-dwelling birds do the same to find their way in the dark. Some even use their sonar to hunt.

Sonar is used by ships and submarines to find the water's depth, map the shape and nature of the seafloor, and locate icebergs, other vessels, wrecks, and even schools of fish.

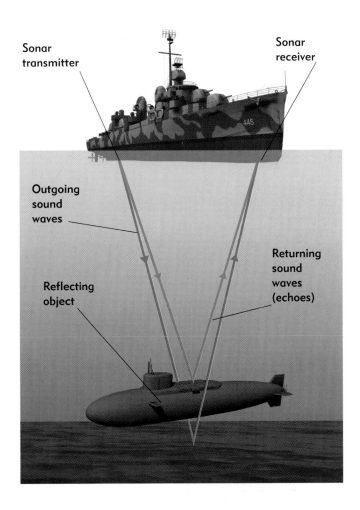

Sonar transmitter

Sonar receiver

Outgoing sound waves

Returning sound waves (echoes)

Reflecting object

SOUND PITCH AND VOLUME

Pitch is how high and squeaky or low and booming a sound is. Sound waves of different frequency—numbers of waves per second—give different pitches of sound. High-frequency sounds have many waves per second and are more high pitched. Low-frequency sounds have few waves per second and are lower pitched and more rumbling.

Sound waves of different amplitude (height) give sounds of different loudness or volume, from shallow-waved whispers to ear-splitting, high-waved roars.

Pitch

Our ears can hear only some of the sounds that exist, because they are able to detect just a limited range of pitches. Like frequencies of light and other waves, these are measured in units called Hertz (Hz). The lowest sounds we can hear are about 20–25 Hz. They include the thump of a bass drum, the growling of thunder, and the deep notes of a bass guitar or double bass.

The highest sounds we can hear are about 18,000–20,000 Hz. They include the trilling of bird song, the shrill "sssss" of a cymbal, and the tinkle of an orchestral triangle. Many animals can detect sounds far beyond the range of human hearing.

A jet plane makes high-amplitude and low-frequency sounds, which means they are loud and deep.

Volume

The loudness, or volume, of a sound is often given in **decibels** (dB). In fact, decibels are really units for measuring the intensity or power of a sound, that is, the amount of energy carried by the sound waves. But for everyday use, the decibel scale is commonly used to describe volume.

A sound almost too quiet to hear, such as a ticking watch, is about 10 dB. Sounds above 120 dB are extremely dangerous, and such sounds cause irreversible damage to the auditory nerve. Many public places, such as concert halls, now have regulations limiting the volume of sound to 90 dB, 85 dB or even less. Being exposed to loud sounds for a long time increases the risk of hearing loss. Where loud sounds are unavoidable, such as at airports and in certain factories, safety regulations insist that people wear ear protection or headphones.

TEST FILE

BOTTLE XYLOPHONE
(You will need a musical instrument, such as a piano or guitar, plus someone who knows how to play it!)

• Put eight identical empty glass bottles (such as lemonade bottles) in a row, about one centimeter (0.4 in.) apart.
• Tap the left one with a spoon and listen carefully to the pitch of the sound it makes. Find the note of the same pitch on the piano or guitar. Let's say it's B on the musical scale.
• Play the next note in the musical scale, which would be C, on the piano or guitar. Tapping the second bottle in the row, gradually pour water into it. Hear how its sound gradually rises in pitch. Stop when the bottle's sound is the same pitch as the musical note.
• Do the same again, working along the row of bottles, for all notes of the musical scale, A to G.
• You can now play a tune on your bottle xylophone. Try this sequence of bottles (1 being the bottle on the far left, with the lowest note):

1 1 5 5 6 7 8 6 5 4 4 3 3 2 2 1

▲ **Even a butterfly's wings make tiny sounds, but too quiet for our ears.**

Mixed sounds

Very few sounds are pure tones, that is, sounds in which all the waves are exactly the same length. Most sounds are mixtures of wavelengths. The main wavelengths are known as dominant tones, while the others are called overtones.

This mixture and balance of dominant tones and overtones, with different frequencies and intensities, is called tonal quality. It is extremely complicated and unique to almost every sound source. It allows us to identify sounds and differentiate between very similar ones, such as a picking out a certain person's voice in a noisy room, and telling the difference between the notes of a flute and a piccolo, or the growls of a lion and a wolf.

◄ **Sounds that are too loud can cause permanent hearing loss.**

UNHEARD SOUNDS

The world is full of sounds, but our ears only pick up a small proportion of them. Sounds that are too low in pitch or frequency for our ears to detect, that is, below about 20 Hz, are called **infrasounds**. If they are loud, like the rumble of a large heavy truck passing or the deepest bass notes of a huge church organ, we can sometimes feel them as a shaking in the ground or in our bodies.

Low-frequency infrasounds travel long distances compared to higher-frequency sounds. Some animals use infrasounds to communicate. In the African bush country, elephants send deep booming infrasound notes to other herd members 2 or 3 kilometers (1.25–2 mi.) away. In the ocean, great whales sing eerie songs to attract mates. Their infrasonic calls can travel hundreds of kilometers through the ocean. The sperm whale can make an extremely loud infrasonic blast to stun nearby animal prey.

Using infrasounds

Special microphones and vibration-detectors are used to pick up infrasonic frequencies, especially from the ground. These are translated into audible sounds or displayed on a screen. They warn of earthquakes or volcanic eruptions, or help to find underground resources of oil, coal, metals, or minerals.

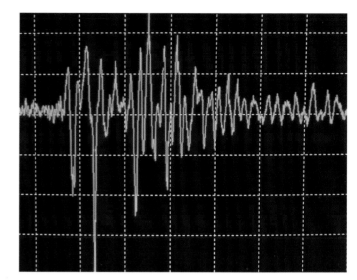

The sound of an earthquake is recorded as part of the pattern of vibrations shown on a seismograph screen.

Humpback whales lie still in the water, flippers drooping, as they sing their songs with whoops and wails.

Some people can hear the very high clicks and squeaks made by bats.

FUTURE FILE

SEEING BY SOUND
One day, it may be possible to fit an echo-location system, like those used by bats, into a headset that could be worn by humans. Incredibly fast sequences of ultrasonic pulses would beam out of the headset, reflect off objects, and return as echoes. As the headset detected the echoes, a small computer would convert the echo pattern into a visible image and display it on a screen in the headset. In this way, we could use sound instead of light to see our way in complete darkness.

Ultrasounds

Sounds that are above about 20,000 Hz—too high in pitch for our ears to detect—are called **ultrasounds**. Like infrasounds, animals use ultrasounds to communicate and also to navigate. Many animals that echolocate (see page 33) use ultrasounds with frequencies up to 250,000 Hz. Some grasshoppers make mating calls of between 50,000 and 100,000 Hz. At about 25,000 Hz, a dog whistle may be silent to us, but it is easily heard by a dog.

Using ultrasounds

Special loudspeakers and vibrating crystals can be made to produce ultrasounds. These have many uses in science, technology, and medicine. Ultrasounds can be focused more easily than lower-frequency sounds to form a narrow and intense beam. This can find defects or flaws in plastic, metal, and other substances.

High-power ultrasound beams will vibrate and heat their targets. They are used to clean away dirt, scour or etch a surface, drill holes, melt and weld, and shatter kidney or bladder stones in the body without the need for surgery. Low-power ultrasound waves beamed into the body are reflected by various body parts, as in sonar. A computer analyzes the echoes and produces a wavy line trace, or image. This method is used to make an echocardiogram image of the heart and an ultrasound scan of a baby in the womb.

Cable to computer and display

Ultrasound probe

Ultrasound waves pass through body

Baby in womb

Echoes of ultrasound return to probe

A growing baby in the womb is checked by an ultrasound scan.

HEARING AND SPEAKING

Most of us think of the human ear as the curved, skin-covered, fleshy funnel on the side of the head. But this is only the outer ear flap, or pinna. A dark hole in the pinna called the ear canal leads along a slightly S-shaped, 25 millimeter- (.039 inch-) long tunnel into the skull. A thin, taut flap of skin, the eardrum, stretches across the end of this tunnel. These three parts—pinna, ear canal, and eardrum—form the outer ear.

Middle ear

When sound waves hit the eardrum, they cause it to vibrate. Behind the eardrum is a thimble-sized air chamber in the skull. Positioned across this chamber, which is called the middle ear cavity, are three tiny bones. The bones are connected to each other by miniature joints. The outer bone, the hammer, is joined to the eardrum. The middle bone is called the anvil and the inner bone the stirrup. Vibrations pass from the eardrum along the row of bones, rattling them like the links of a chain.

Ear canal

Semicircular canals (balance)

Auditory nerve

Ear bones

Cochlea

Eardrum

Ear flap

The delicate parts deep in the ear change sound waves to nerve signals.

Hairs sticking up from cells in the cochlea are rocked by sound vibrations.

Inner ear

The base of the stirrup bone is joined to the **cochlea**, a fluid-filled tube that looks like a little snail. As the stirrup vibrates against the side of the cochlea, the vibrations ripple through fluid inside it. They shake the tectorial membrane, which is a long, thin sheet coiled inside the cochlea's tube.

The surface of the tectorial membrane is covered with more than one million tiny hairs that stick out from about 23,000 microscopic hair cells. As the membrane vibrates, it pulls on these hairs, and makes their cells generate tiny electrical nerve signals.

The nerve signals pass from the cochlea and along the auditory nerve to the two hearing or auditory centers on the sides of the brain. Here they are analyzed and compared with information in the brain's memory, so the sounds can be identified.

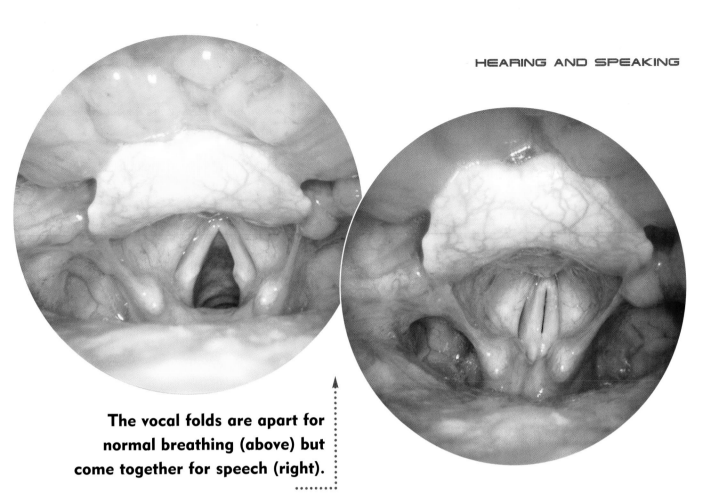

The vocal folds are apart for normal breathing (above) but come together for speech (right).

 **TEST FILE**

THE TALKING BALLOON
A balloon shows how vocal cords work.
• Blow it up carefully. Grip the neck tightly between the forefinger and thumb of each hand, and stretch the neck wide. Adjust the tension until air leaks slowly out of the balloon and makes a squeaking noise.
• The two sides of the neck are like vocal cords, with air passing between them. The balloon itself is like the lungs, forcing air past the cords.
• Stretch the neck tighter. The squeaking should rise in pitch. This is like the larynx muscles pulling the vocal cords tighter, to make your voice higher-pitched.
• Get a friend to squash the balloon, to make air come out faster. The squeak should get louder. This is like your lungs pushing air more forcefully past the vocal cords, to make your voice louder.

The human voice

Crying, laughter, whispers, bellows, speech, songs—these sounds are all called vocalizations. They come from the **larynx**, or voice-box, in the neck. The larynx is a tunnel-like arrangement of gristly plates, between the bottom of the throat and the top of the windpipe. It contains two vocal cords, one on either side. Despite their name, the cords are not strings, like those of a guitar or violin. They are actually folds or flaps of tough skin that stick out from the sides of the larynx.

Vocal sounds

Normally the vocal cords have a wide V-gap between them, through which air passes in and out of the lungs during breathing. To make sounds, muscles pull the cords together so there is only a tiny slit between them. As air passes through the slit, it causes the cords to vibrate and make sound waves.

Muscles around the larynx stretch the vocal cords tighter to make higher-pitched sounds, while muscles in the chest make the lungs breathe out more forcefully to produce louder sounds. The tongue, lips, and pharynx (the upper throat) then form the sounds into words.

39

FROM SOUND TO ELECTRICITY

Musical instruments work by making the air vibrate in a regular fashion that is pleasing to the ear. Musicians play tunes and make rhythms by controlling the amplitude and frequency of the vibrations produced by their instruments.

When sound waves hit an object, the object may pick up their energy and vibrate at the same frequency as the sound waves. The vibrating object produces yet more sound waves, making the sound seem louder and richer. This is called resonance.

Many musical instruments use resonance. The hollow, thin body of a violin or guitar is set vibrating by sound waves from the strings, adding to the overall sound. Instruments that rely on natural sound waves like this—from flutes and trumpets to pianos and drums—are known as acoustic instruments. Acoustic instruments can be made louder using electrical equipment such as microphones, amplifiers, and loudspeakers.

 FACT FILE

THE DOPPLER EFFECT

When a sound source moves in relation to the listener, the pitch (frequency) of the sound alters.

• If the sound source moves towards the listener, the pitch gets higher, because the sound waves bunch together in front of it and increase in frequency.

• If the sound source moves away from the listener, the pitch gets lower, because the sound waves spread out behind it and decrease in frequency.

• This effect is familiar with cars, trains, planes, and other fast-moving vehicles. The noise they make becomes lower as they go past. This change in pitch is also very noticeable in the sirens of passing police cars and ambulances.

• It is called the Doppler effect, after the Austrian physicist Christian Doppler (1803–53), who first described it.

• The Doppler effect works with any type of wave, not just sound.

• In light, the Doppler effect causes a phenomenon called red-shift. The light from many stars and galaxies is redder (has a lower frequency) than astronomers expect. This shows that the stars and galaxies are moving away from Earth and the whole universe, which is already infinite, is getting bigger!

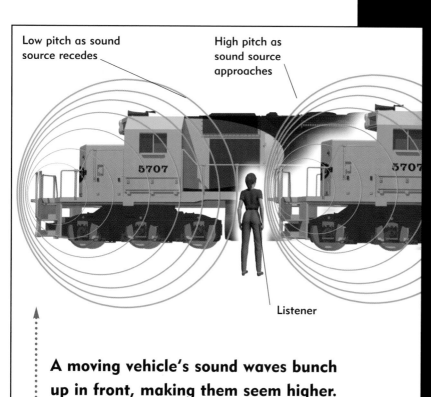

Low pitch as sound source recedes

High pitch as sound source approaches

Listener

A moving vehicle's sound waves bunch up in front, making them seem higher.

5707

Copying sound waves

As sound waves from a musical instrument enter a microphone, they hit a diaphragm, a thin, flexible sheet, something like the eardrum. The diaphragm is fixed to a coil of thin wire next to a magnet. When sound waves hit the diaphragm, it vibrates within the magnet's force field. This causes pulses, or signals, of electricity to flow through the wire. The pattern of electrical signals copies the pattern of the sound waves.

From the microphone, the electrical signals travel along wires to an amplifier that boosts their strength. The signals then pass along more wires to a loudspeaker.

Reproducing sound waves

A loudspeaker has a diaphragm, or speaker cone, attached to a wire coil that is positioned close to a magnet. Electrical signals pass through the coil of thin wire and create a varying magnetic field around the coil. This field interacts with the force field of the magnet, pushing and pulling the coil, and causing it to vibrate. The vibrating coil makes the diaphragm vibrate, too, producing sound waves in the surrounding air. The pattern of sound waves matches the patterns originally copied by the microphone.

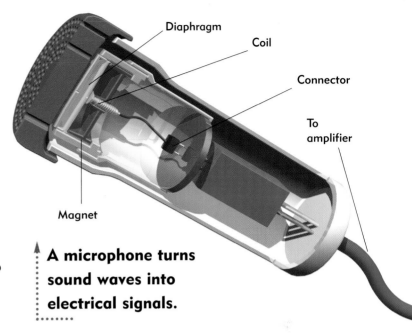

Diaphragm
Coil
Connector
To amplifier
Magnet

A microphone turns sound waves into electrical signals.

A loudspeaker has a similar construction to a microphone, but it works in the opposite way.

Loudspeaker for high sounds

Loudspeaker for low sounds

Magnet

Coil

Sound-directing plates (baffles)

TEST FILE

BEATS

Gradually tune two strings of an acoustic guitar to nearly the same note—in other words, the same pitch or frequency. Pluck both strings together as you tune them. As the notes become more similar, the combined sound from the strings seems to form one note that regularly rises and falls in volume. These pulses of volume are called beats. They are the result of interference (see page 28) between two sounds with slightly different wavelengths. They repeatedly nearly cancel each other out and become quieter, and then gradually add together and become louder again, and so on.

USING SOUND SIGNALS

Electrical signals can be altered in many more ways than sound waves can. Once a pattern of sound waves is changed into a corresponding pattern of electrical signals by a microphone, the signals can be made shorter, longer, bigger, smaller, sharper, rounder, and so on. This creates new and different sounds when the signals are played back through a loudspeaker.

Storing sounds

Electrical sound signals can be stored in a variety of different forms and then played back at a later date. One way of storing these signals is as a spiraling, wavy groove cut into the surface of a vinyl disk. To play the sound back, a sharp stylus, or needle, runs along the groove as the disk spins on a turntable. The groove's wavy shape makes the stylus vibrate. A device called a pick-up, just above the stylus, converts the vibrations into electrical signals that can then be fed to an amplifier and loudspeaker.

A compact disk, or CD, stores the signals as a spiral track of microscopic pits in its shiny surface. Inside a CD player, a laser beam is focused on the surface as the disk spins. The beam reflects off flat areas between the pits but not off the pits

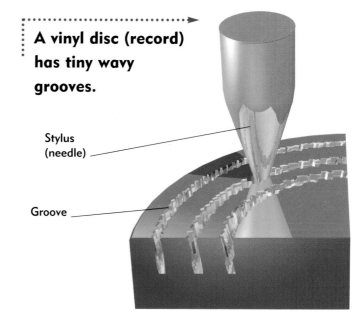

A vinyl disc (record) has tiny wavy grooves.

Stylus (needle)

Groove

themselves. This produces a code of flashing reflections that is detected by a sensor and converted back into electrical signals.

Electrical sound signals can also be stored as tiny patches of magnetism on a tape or disk coated with magnetic material. In a magnetic tape or disk player, a "read" head containing a tiny coil of wire detects these patches as the tape moves past and changes them into electrical signals once again.

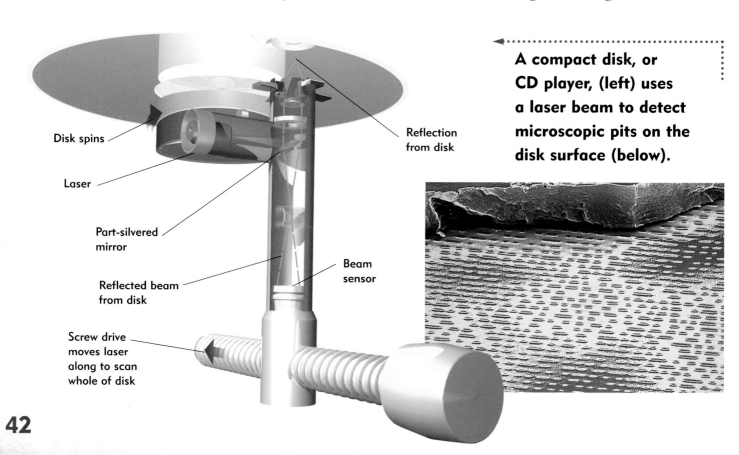

Disk spins

Laser

Part-silvered mirror

Reflected beam from disk

Screw drive moves laser along to scan whole of disk

Reflection from disk

Beam sensor

A compact disk, or CD player, (left) uses a laser beam to detect microscopic pits on the disk surface (below).

Some acoustic instruments have been electrified for greater sound projection.

Electrical instruments

Acoustic instruments make their own sounds. Electric instruments make little or no sounds themselves. They produce electrical signals instead. These signals are fed into an amplifier and then into a loudspeaker, to produce sound waves. Electric instruments include electric guitars, electric pianos, and electric drums.

Complete control

The synthesizer is an electronic device that generates its own electrical sound signals. A synthesizer can create a vast range of sounds, copy existing musical instruments or other sound sources, take snatches or samples of existing recordings, and even invent completely new types of sounds. It can squash, stretch, bend, cut, and tilt sound waves in all kinds of ways. The combination of a synthesizer and a computer gives complete control over sound waves in their electronic form before they are replayed through a loudspeaker.

In a recording studio, sounds are altered and mixed, but they are in electrical, not acoustic, form.

FUTURE FILE

BIONIC SIGHTS AND SOUNDS

Electronics and medicine may soon be able to help people who cannot see, hear, or talk in the normal way.
• A microchip implanted in the eye could help people with sight problems to have better vision. The microchip would contain CCDs (see page 25) that convert light energy into electrical signals and send them to the brain, just as the nerve cells of the retina do in a normal eye.
• A microchip in the ear could improve the hearing of people with partial deafness. The microchip would convert sound waves into electrical signals and send them to the brain, just as the cochlea's nerve cells do in normal hearing.
• A microchip and vibrating plate in the voicebox could help people with speech problems to talk more clearly. The microchip would receive electrical nerve signals from the brain and use them to control the speed and size of the plate's vibrations, so that it worked like ordinary vocal cords.

GLOSSARY

Cochlea The part of the ear where the energy of sound waves is turned into nerve signals and sent to the brain.

Decibel A measurement of the amount of energy in a sound, which is usually similar to its loudness or volume.

Echo A sound that bounces off a hard, smooth surface, so that the ears hear it just after the original sound, but more faintly.

Electromagnetic radiation Energy that travels as waves of electrical and magnetic fields.

Energy The ability to cause changes or make things happen or do work. Energy comes in many forms, including light, sound, electricity, heat, and movement.

Focus The point at which light rays come together after passing through a lens or bouncing off a curved mirror.

Frequency The number of waves going past a place in one second, or the number of waves in a certain distance.

Hertz A measurement of the frequency of a wave or vibration. One hertz is equivalent to one wave per second.

Hologram An image produced by a laser on a flat, two dimensional surface, but which seems to have three dimensions—with depth as well as height and width—so that you can see all round it.

Infrasounds Sounds too low in pitch or frequency for our ears to detect.

Interference The way that waves combine and either become stronger or cancel each other out.

Larynx The voice box in the neck, where the vocal cords vibrate to make sounds.

Laser A special kind of intense, high-energy light in which all the rays are the same color and do not spread out from each other.

Polarized light Light in which all the waves undulate in the same direction, such as straight up and down, rather than undulating in many different directions.

Reflection The way light rays bounce off surfaces.

Refraction The way light rays bend as they move from one substance to another.

Retina The thin lining in the rear of the eyeball, where the energy of light rays is turned into nerve signals that are sent to the brain.

Spectrum The range of colors obtained by splitting up ordinary white light.

Ultrasounds Sounds too high in pitch or frequency for our ears to detect.

Vacuum A place where there is nothing, not even air or specks of dust.

Vibration A rapid back-and-forth movement around a central or middle point.

Wavelength The distance from a point on one wave to the same point on the next wave, such as from one crest to the next crest.

FURTHER INFORMATION

FURTHER READING

Ardley, Neil. *Light* (Way It Works series). Simon and Schuster Childrens, 2001.

Drews, Mark. New Ears: The Audio Career and Education Handbook. New Ear Productions, 1993.

Kerrod, Robin. *Light and Sound* (Let's Investigate Science series). Marshall Cavendish, 1995.

Lauber, Patricia. *What Do You See?* Random House Value, 1998.

Morgan, Sally and Adrian Morgan. *Using Light* (Designs in Science series). Facts on File, 1993.

Rosen, Sibyl, and Cliff Nielsen. *Speed of Light*. Atheneum, Simon and Schuster Childrens, 1999.

WEB SITES

http://sln.fi.edu/tfi/hotlists/kid-sci.html
Franklin Institute Science Museum

http://www.hhmi.org/senses/a/a130.htm
Franklin Institute Science Museum. Resources include: information on the senses, including seeing and hearing.

http://education.gsfc.nasa.gov/
Technology information. Hubble space telescope.

http://www.eastman.org
History of photography, collections, and overview of the technology.

http://synthmuseum.com/index.html
Electronic musical instruments from all over the world.

http://es.rice.edu:80/ES/humsoc/Galileo/Things/telescope.html
A history of the telescope.

INDEX

The Electromagnetic Spectrum

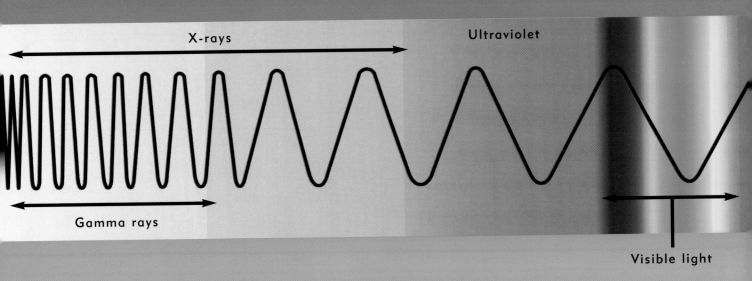

X-rays

Ultraviolet

Gamma rays

Visible light

SPEED OF LIGHT AND REFRACTIVE INDEX

Material	Speed	Refractive Index (how much the material refracts light)
Air	300.000 km (984 ft) /s⁻¹	1.00
Water	225,000 km (740,000 ft) /s⁻¹	1.33
Acrylic plastic	210,000 km (689,000 ft) /s⁻¹	1.40
Glass (variable)	185,000 km (607,000 ft) /s⁻¹	1.60
Diamond	125,000 km (410,105 ft) /s⁻¹	2.40

Decibel Scale

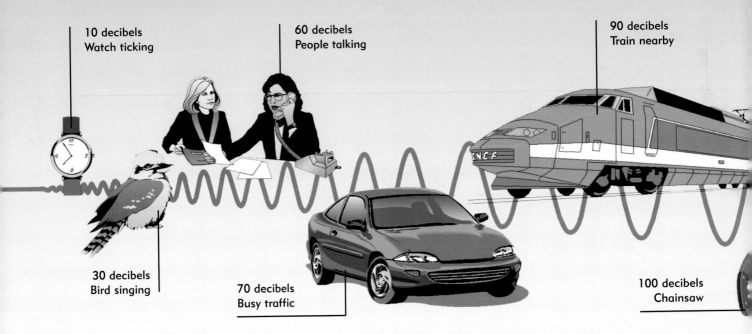

10 decibels
Watch ticking

60 decibels
People talking

90 decibels
Train nearby

30 decibels
Bird singing

70 decibels
Busy traffic

100 decibels
Chainsaw

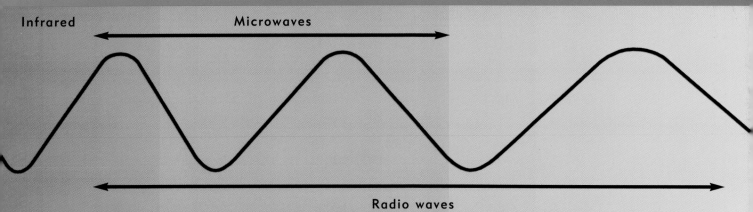

Infrared

Microwaves

Radio waves

MAKING AND HEARING SOUNDS (frequency in Hertz)

Animal	Sounds it makes	Sounds it hears
Human	85–1,100 Hz	20–20,000 Hz
Dog	450–1,080 Hz	15–50,000 Hz
Cat	700–1,600 Hz	60–60,000 Hz
Grasshopper	7,000–100,000 Hz	100–15,000 Hz
Bat	10,000–120,000 Hz	1,000–120,000 Hz

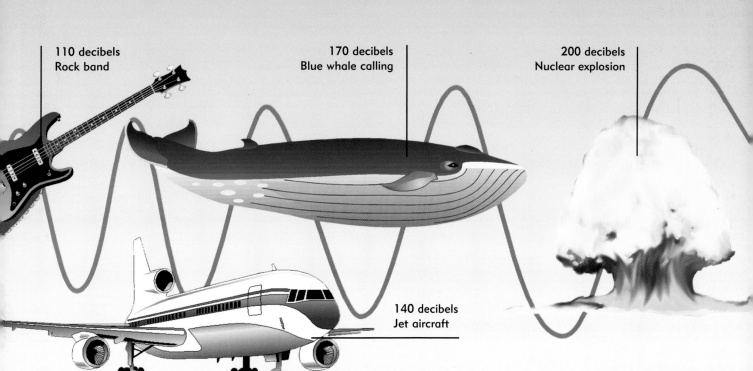

110 decibels
Rock band

170 decibels
Blue whale calling

200 decibels
Nuclear explosion

140 decibels
Jet aircraft

CODMAN SQUARE

9